What I Did For Pizza

A Field Guide for Investment, and Uncertainty

William Haigh

ISBN 978-1-7645069-0-8 (Paperback)

ISBN 978-1-7645069-1-5 (Hardcover)

Published by Couching About

First published in Australia

First edition, 2026

Dedicated to Will, Keith, Sean & Tyson.

The best friends I could ask for.

Special dedication to my Mother.

This book would never have been possible without her.

Disclaimer

This book is written for general information and educational purposes only. It is not financial, investment, tax, or legal advice, and I am not a licensed financial adviser. Nothing in this book is a recommendation to buy/sell/hold any financial product. Everything shared here reflects personal experience, observations, and lessons learned, not instructions or recommendations. All investing involves risk, including the risk of loss, and no outcomes, past, present, or future, are guaranteed. Markets change, rules change, and circumstances differ from person to person. This book is written from an Australian perspective, and laws or tax obligations may vary depending on where you live. Any decisions you make are your own, and you should consider your personal situation and seek independent professional advice where appropriate. Any examples used in this book are illustrative only and not intended to be followed or replicated. This book does not consider your personal objectives, financial situation, or needs. It should be stated that the information in this book is in no way all encompassing. Further research may be required. Above all, this book is a guide to mindset and understanding, not certainty. If you're unsure, talk to a licensed financial adviser or accountant before acting.

Table Of Contents

Foreword/Introduction

Pizza. It's Schrödinger's food, topped with the good, the bad, and the ugly. Healthy and unhealthy at the same time, which is why I chose it as my ultimate goal. I found it a fitting example of what I was going to do; change my future in an uncertain world.

Years ago, I was desperate to change my circumstances to the point I would risk myself and the sustainability of my lifestyle. But this is not a lesson in failure; it's a lesson in growth, the future, sustainability, and a tiny bit of maths. Risk is inherent in life and there will be times when you don't succeed as much as you would like but choosing whether you learn and grow from those risks is optional.

This is why I implore you to read this book. This is a book about investment but ultimately this book is more about knowing yourself and accepting, celebrating, and when it happens, forgiving your actions as you take them.

This book isn't for the middle class, or the upper class, it's for everyone. It's about carving a small financial crevice in the world that is your own. You may not be wealthy by the end of it but it may help with retirement, leave something to your family or friends, or if you decide to dive deep well past this book it might give you a few dollars pocket money (or none at all).

Everything I tell you in this book is drawn from hard-learned lessons and scars. There will be days you may be unsure of yourself but if you understand, and absorb the information inside these pages, it may help prepare you for what comes.

I won't promise the world. I'm not a magician, scientist, or artist, neither are these skills. It's understanding. All I will provide is education, and a chance to add something to your financial life in this world of increasing geopolitical instability, and inequity.

Because I'm expressing my path to my personal future; I must preface, this may be working for me but the future is undefined. Use this as a guide and nothing more.

But there is one thing in this book you do need to pay attention to: you must be kind to yourself no matter what.

If you end up finding this book useful and you have adult children, consider gifting a copy to them. It may end up sitting on a shelf for 10 years but the lessons in this could guide them well into the future. If they decide to open the pages one day… well let's see what this book has to say first.

Oh… by the way, when I talk about "getting started" or "being ready", I mean mentally and educationally, not that you should take action now, or at all. It's all about your preparedness, and your confidence.

Notes On Reading This Book

Reading this book, you may come across sub-chapters. These are considered additional or expanded information. They often cover important topics which may not have been included in the main chapter or may have been glossed over.

Every chapter has a main chapter and sometimes sub-chapters with the exception of Chapter 4 which is all sub-chapters, which I recommend you read as it covers many dense and important topics.

Take your time reading this book. It's a light read but it covers many abstract topics which may require thought.

You got this.

Why Advice Sounds Universal but Isn’t

If you’ve come here looking for a predefined and formulated strategy this book isn’t for you.

This book is for those who want to learn the lessons that others don’t teach, who are willing to use the guidance in this book and do it themselves.

I don’t provide any financial advice in this book. I do provide trains of thought, personal examples, and concepts which should be considered before investing or trading.

Why do I do this? Advice sounds universal but isn’t. After years of trading on a variety of markets, both highly risky, and well… maybe still risky. I can say for certain that no one plan fits all, and the only plan that can work is one you’ve designed and are comfortable with. So sit down, grab a cup of tea or coffee, and relax. We have some pages to read.

Concept Index

The following terms are used throughout this book. They are descriptive explanations of how markets and behaviour function, not instructions or recommendations.

Ape brain: The part of your brain that your ancestors evolved to survive in the wild. Reactionary, and chaotic.

Human brain: The brain you use in your day-to-day life. Logical and calm.

Thesis: A document detailing how to react, and respond to different events with a single stock and/or trade.

Strategy: Your basic rules, and instructions you set yourself on how to trade. You can have multiple strategies.

Revenue: How much money the company has made.

Earnings: How much money the company has made after costs.

Liquidity: How easily a stock can be bought or sold without significantly affecting its price.

Slippage: The difference between the expected trade price and the price at which the order actually fills.

Volatility: How much and how quickly a stock's price moves over time.

Spread: The difference between the bid and ask price.

Drawdown: The decline from a peak price to a lower point.

Market Adaptation: When strategies lose effectiveness as more participants use them.

Confirmation Bias: The tendency to seek information that supports existing beliefs.

Loss Aversion: The tendency to feel losses more strongly than gains.

Diversification: Spreading investments across assets or industries to reduce risk.

These concepts are intentionally simplified. Precision comes from how you apply them together, not from any single definition.

Chapter 1 – The Pizza Gambit

One of the universal parts of life is the desire for reward after action. This exists in almost everything we do. The thing we sometimes miss is that not everything should require an immediate reward.

When I started trading my focus was on short-term gains in order to make a large profit, something which creates a lot of stress, and in turn encourages you to make mistakes. Not everyone can handle that. It was not until I tried my hand at forex, day trading on the stock market, and crypto that I sat down and listen to the advice of a friend. “Play the long game.” Now, I never truly believed that such an action would be viable (or even fun) but after I sat down and did the maths. Well… it ended up clearing my head of idealism and false hope.

Now I’m not saying that day trading is for no one but it’s certainly not for everyone. And best of all, you don’t even need to be a mathematical genius to slowly and carefully build your wealth. Just an understanding of what some numbers mean and what they mean in the market (which I will tell you later). Once you’re set up, you may want to spend at most 30 minutes a day on this. That’s all you may need to do, and that’s being liberal. Really, you don’t need to spend that much time at all. Just keep an eye on things.

So let’s start the learning process; I’m going to start with the three most important things you need when building your wealth.

1. Kindness
2. Patience
3. Discipline

Kindness for yourself and when you make mistakes. Perfection is a myth in life should it be any different with finances?

Patience to grow. Don’t expect a turn around immediately. Wealth, and experience take time.

Discipline to invest. Regular contributions and reinvesting matter more than fast returns. Wealth builds with time and consistency. Even if you reach a snowball where your contributions are too small to matter, you may want to continue to add contributions. Such action will keep your mind in the right state, and help you continue to grow.

This leads me to the pizza gambit.

Once I had realised that the future was not in the short term and only if I took my time, my family and friends made a deal. Invest 5k by year’s end and we’ll go out for a high-quality pizza. Invest 10k and we’ll make pizzas from scratch. What would the pizza look like over 10k? Homemade dough, sauce, and toppings in a pizza oven. Everyone would chip in. Not a bad option. At the time it felt a little shallow. I was expecting a big reward. Especially since 10k was a third of my yearly income (which I don’t think is a good idea in retrospect). But then I realised. No, that is the perfect reward. I like pizza. I **LOVE** pizza and in order to make that target I would have to reduce my pizza intake. A shame for sure, but also a compromise I was willing to make.

The great thing about the pizza gambit is that it is such a token prize. No pressure to make that level of investment. Just motivation. If that pressure existed, I would make riskier and riskier trades to reach that level. That's just not a good idea.

So that's what I'm suggesting now. If you're ready to go down your own path into the stock market find something you can reward yourself with for meeting your goals at the end of the year. Something meaningful but inconsequential. Like pizza.

With that said, I would encourage you to set achievable goals. For most people, a third of your yearly income is not an achievable goal. When I set that goal there was a source of desperation to plan for my retirement. It's not that simple. There are many methods to reach your goals. Some take experience and scars, others (and the better ones in my opinion) take kindness, discipline and patience. Those are the ones you might want to start as soon as possible. It's the potential difference between living on a pension and living on the pension with most of your rent taken care of. Not glamorous, but in my opinion extremely essential. Heck, if you start in your 20s there may be a good chance you'll be able to retire on your investments. But alas, there are often many other bigger priorities in your 20s than your retirement but it's something people may consider.

Chapter 2 – Understanding: The Art of Doing Nothing and Something

Here we start to dig into the nitty-gritty stuff. The understanding and lessons pushed forth by years of action. Big lessons with big meanings, that lesson being effort does not necessarily mean profit, and action does not mean smart. Doing nothing is a completely valid action and one that you may decide to consider on a daily basis. Note inaction does not mean complacency. That's like putting a jar of fish flakes in the fish bowl and telling the fish to feed itself. You have to care and feed the fish just not feed it every hour of the day.

So what do I mean?

Well, I'm going to give you an example.

You've been putting money aside every paycheck. You have a nice little cash safety net and some left over in a little bank account for investing. You choose a nice safe stock you know won't disappear on you even in the worst of times. But you are aware enough to know nothing is too big to fail. A financial crisis hits. You see red numbers on the news every night. But you understand what you're seeing is temporary. You look at your shares weekly, and see that even though the traders are crying the company you invested in is hurting but holding strong. You do nothing.

That is the art of doing nothing. While this is not the only strategy to take in a financial crisis (we will be going over ways to ease the pain of crashes later in this book) it is a perfectly valid one. It is the ability to say no to fear for long term gain.

Quite often in this book I will be using silly terms like ape brain and human brain. Simply put they are parts of you that evolution has refined, honed, and quite honestly perfected. However, none of them are trained for modern day markets. That's something you will have to do yourself.

But, as shown above, market collapses often triggers the ape brain's loss aversion. But usually by this point, retail traders, like you and me, will suffer the most, we will make a loss, and exit the market out of fear. Yet there are sometimes ways to take advantage of market crashes and come out faster than your peers who took and ran.

This leads to the art of doing something. Knowing when to do it and why to do it. With that said, the art of doing nothing is much more important.

Using the example of a market crash again. There are times when it may be very risky but also viable to do nothing by doing something.

Assuming you invest weekly, like I do, and then a crash happens, do nothing and continue to invest. What? The market is going down? I'm losing money? No. You might not. You're making an intentional choice to continue with your investments like always. Not only is this better for the economy. It's also a potentially viable but risky strategy. It's called "down-averaging". If the company is solid and there's no sign of it disappearing as you watch it carefully from the sidelines you can in some cases invest more. As you do so, you will be buying shares at a lower price and with a lower P/E (we'll cover that later, don't worry for now). Each share you buy may average out over time and as the market begins to rise again you'll have more and better value stocks than if you bought them at a high. You will lose money. Everyone does in a crash. It's about how fast you might come out ahead of the pack.

Imagine it like this. You're in a foot race. You're keeping up with everyone else but you know you and everyone else is running out of steam. If you drop back and recover you know you have the chance to sprint the final leg faster than the people maintaining their current speed. That's what you're aiming to do. Recover ground in the final leg where everyone is flailing.

It's not a perfect analogy but it's good enough for this.

Just note that if your thesis about the company you invest in is wrong this can magnify your losses. Told you it was risky.

But, this is the art of doing nothing by doing something.

Note: I don't recommend down-averaging for everyone. That's something you'll have to research yourself, and decide on yourself. It can also be psychologically stressful, and draining.

Now, with all of this said, we've got to have the plain old art of doing something.

That's easy: it's knowing when to act but it's also the biggest trap. That's your ape brain again telling you you're always right. Otherwise known as confirmation bias. No investor or trader is without it. Learning how to challenge your ape brain with your human brain is the skill you will have to learn. Sadly, that is not one that can be taught with words but with experience. Which is where kindness, patience, and discipline come into play.

Mistakes happen. I still make trades which don't go in my favour but I follow my rules and strategy and I may slowly come out on top. Speaking of which, what are those rules and strategies? Should I tell you? Eh. Probably not. You cannot rely on a strategy you haven't formed yourself. You can try but fundamental misunderstandings can occur because as you develop your own strategy, intricacies form that sometimes can be put into words but other times not. A strategy isn't a feeling, it's a set of rules you define for yourself and you follow without bias.

Regardless, I will put some steps which may partially form a bare bones strategy in the next chapter. These should be used as information only, and you may want to write your own to suit your circumstances.

Chapter 3 – The Strategy – Or How I Learnt To Ignore Everything in this Book

OK. You're sitting there thinking "OK, I'm listening but not convinced." Good. I don't want you to be. Nothing sends danger signals off when a book pretends to solve all your questions in the first 2 chapters.

Let's talk about starting the process, let's start about forming some thoughts that can help you with your strategy.

Step 1:

Know what you're getting into. You're getting into a psychological minefield. Are you prepared? No? Good. You're in the right mindset. You will never be prepared. I don't mean to scare you off but money is something that worries people for good reason. It's a metaphor for sustainability in our globalised world. Read the previous chapter again and be prepared for things to go wrong, things to look bad, or just be nervous. That's perfectly natural. Once you accept that, you're ready for step two.

Step 2: Set aside Step 1

Have you accepted that? Good. Now set aside step one in the back of your brain and understand that sustainability is made through learning from your mistakes, be kind when you mess up. If you sell and make a loss, that's fine. You had a good reason even if that reason was fear. Forgive yourself and keep on learning. Human nature is to grow. Fear will only inhibit that growth if you don't show yourself kindness. Easier said than done but it's a skill you will learn.

Step 3: Prepare

Save what you can per paycheck. Put it aside in an account. Save as much as you need but don't rush it. Have a safety net for yourself before investing in the stock market. I made that mistake early, putting all my spare money into shares. While it grew my portfolio slightly quicker, it didn't make a long term difference except when I was under financial stress. Take your time. The market will always have new opportunities. Remember, financial stress changes behaviour, and behaviour, not markets, is usually what causes damage.

Ultimately, it's up to you how you save and invest your money.

Step 4: Understand the technicals and fundamentals (the next chapters)

These are the boring chapters, it'll be long, slightly (but not really) maths-based and will cover a few different things to pay attention to in order to know when and how to trade.

Step 5: Breathe and Invest (another chapter)

You've taken the first step. You've researched and found a reliable broker that meets your needs. You've done it. Learn some more and get ready.

Step 6: Continue to invest with weekly revisits.

Invest when you can if you want. Once a week or month check you may want to check everything is good and still meets your thesis. That's covered in the next chapter as well. But always remember, checking too often doesn't make you informed, it can make you reactive. Remember the art of doing nothing.

Step 7: Maintain the 3 principles

Kindness, patience, and discipline

Step 8: Simplify your life (Optional chapter)

This is something I was hesitant to add as I don't want to tell people how to run their lives. It's not my style. I understand everyone's circumstances are different, and the small wins and things make life worth living but if you decide to go a little zen (ok not really) it may be worth a read.

Just note: If this chapter makes you uncomfortable, that's a good sign.

These steps are not what a strategy looks like. These are just informational steps which can provide you with things to consider. In fact in my experience for a retail trader, a strategy has no set form. Just what suits you best.

It should be noted that if you decide to incorporate those steps it's up to you how you do it. That's just my historical guide for myself.

Also, if you’re reading this book for certainty, you’re in the wrong place. If you’re reading it to build resilience, continue on.

I Got 99 Problems But A Thesis Aint One

The stock market is like a rap battle with nerds, we think we know what we're doing, but we're always making mistakes.

How can you reduce the potential risk of mistakes? A thesis. This links into strategy. Strategy is how you make, organise, plan, and make your trades. A thesis is how you know where, when, why, and how you enter or exit your trades.

A strategy or thesis is not a guide to infinite money, just a risk reduction strategy.

We talk about fundamental and technical analysis in the next chapter. These are usually your bread, and butter of a thesis. You may want to use technical indicators to help you decide where to buy in, and you may want to use fundamental analysis for determining whether the company is worth investing in or not.

That said, as I mentioned, you may want to also add some rules in your thesis about exits, when, and how. Writing your trades in a journal is often a good idea used by many traders.

Write these down on paper or in a Word document if you want to. It's what I do. I find it handy having them in a material or semi-material form.

You may be looking for a format right now to base this off. I could provide a template, but it could be much better if one evolves around you, and your style. One that you understand, and one that is uniquely you. You're probably not reading this book if you're a professional trader. Just having your thesis on paper will probably be good enough.

Wait a minute. There's an old proverb. Rules were made to be broken and that's true in the stock market as well. Rules feel safe. They really do. You think if you stick to your rules you'll be fine. Honestly? This is mostly true until it isn't. That's when you may want to rethink your strategy and/or thesis, or your stake in that company. Rules may fail loudly with an obvious change in your thesis, or quietly as you lose money, that's difficult.

I understand. In that instant you may want to take a break, or consider talking to an independent adviser. It's up to you what you do, but know it may take years to see whether a strategy has failed or not.

Sometimes markets change and your strategy is no longer valid. This is quite common. Which is why reviewing your strategy and thesis every fortnight or month may be a good idea. In fact, in my opinion it's a smart idea. These rules are meant to keep you on track not turn you into a rigid rule following robot.

Lastly, usually over-optimising, extrapolating numbers, and over-factoring in market instability is generally considered a bad thing. Not only may it cause financial harm, but psychological harm which I am deliberately trying to avoid with this book.

Why Copying Works Until It Doesn’t

“Pssst, hey Pete. What’s the answer to #3”

Copying, seems like the easiest way to do something sometimes. But it doesn’t always work especially in stock markets.

Enter copy trading, something many people try to do as a short cut to the stock market, or to delegate responsibility to help with the strains of trading. But it doesn’t always work as expected.

Copy trading is simply trading using other peoples exact trades. So if someone makes a trade you make it a split second later. This has many issues in a fast paced market.

People, and machines on the stock market are smart these days, and they may be able adapt to any copy trading done. This is called market adaptation. Once enough people join in on a copy traders strategy the market may adapt and the profitability may disappear.

Second, you may not make an immediate trade, it could take a few milliseconds to whole seconds to get the trade and execute it. Meaning you could miss the trade entirely.

Third, you have no control, over the trades and how they are placed. A simple mistake could cost you a lot of money, as many copy trading strategies which look great have high margins, large drawdowns.

I'll just say this. I think copy trading is a terrible idea. But you do your own research, and if you desire make your own decisions. I understand it may seem like a perfect fit for you on the surface but delegating responsibility is not for everyone. If you do decide to go down this path you may want to talk to an independent financial adviser or accountant.

The Comfort of Having No Answer

Nothing changed, why did that fall? It didn't even break my thesis. Heh. That's happened.

Sometimes you'll never know the answer to many questions you'll have. Sometimes focusing on the obtuse is just a drain of energy. Some questions will never have any response.

That's OK. That's the time you take your time, and refocus yourself. No answer doesn't mean you shouldn't divest or reinvest but it should be another data point whether the price has risen or fallen. I have spent weeks researching into why a company decided to play silly games. That was time I should have spent wisely instead of stressing. The lessons learnt...

This is something you might want to consider adding to your strategy. It's something subtle, often missed, but potentially useful.

When you let it go it's time to move on and invest. Keeping your mind calm is more important than the numbers. Numbers often react badly to a chaotic mind.

Your Attention Is Limited and You Don't Even Have ADHD

Don't look at that. Really, don't. You're focusing too much on it. Whoops. That's what I'm doing with this book.

With the stock market however, it can be better not to look at it. The markets love when you constantly monitor something.

Sometimes when trading your ape brain may tickle your "I'm smart section" of your brain or your "the absolute horror section". This may be triggered or amplified by paying close attention to the numbers going up or down. As the numbers change you might react to them. If you're watching them for fun, and not reacting to them, that's fine. You should just be aware of what can happen if you focus on them too hard.

On the flip side, being complacent doesn't help either. Writing what you're going to do if things aren't looking good on a daily basis in your strategy and/or thesis may be a good idea (when you get round to one).

How you manage your attention can matter more than capital loss itself. The market plays silly games, you have to run your own race amongst the clown show.

Hello World, This Is Me

My sister contaminated my brain with the theme song to an old horse TV show. I don't expect anyone reading this book to remember that corny show. But it's stuck in my mind and to a point my identity.

Sadly, now as writing this sentence, I can't get it out of my mind.

Regardless, it leads to something people should be aware of. Identity contamination.

What does that mean? Well, simply it's when investments stop being decisions and start being part of who you are.

I'll be honest, this is something I'm working on right now.

I like watching investments rise, and fall, I like making them, and I like researching companies in my free time.

The question is when is that healthy, and when does that lead to over analysis, attention mismanagement, attachment, difficulties with loss, and burnout.

Right now I'd say I'm on the border of healthy, and unhealthy. I know this so I'm taking more time to do other things. Like this book. But that's probably taking me more into the unhealthy section. The important difference is I'm not giving too much attention to the market anymore, and as I type this I'm learning more about myself.

These are the sort of things you might want to consider when trading, and you find it encroaching into yourself.

Making your identity trading can encourage many of the bad psychological habits discussed in this book, and as such you should be aware.

Hey, at least I'm trying somewhat, but once this book is done, I will need to transition away from this being part of my identity.

Be healthy, and have a life. Plus people don't like it when you talk trading all day. I realised that fairly early on.

You’ve Done It!

If you’ve gotten this far, you’re doing great! We’ve covered some important topics here, and we’re going to go much deeper now.

The topics we’ll cover will be information-dense, but you can do it! You’ve got this!

It’s time to challenge you further. We’re just getting to the serious stuff. :)

Chapter 4 – White Bread and Mayonnaise

Introduction – Paperclips and Mayo Sandwiches

Would you like a white bread and mayonnaise sandwich? The eternal question when you're as boring as me. However, boring is not a bad thing when building a future. The sad thing is, that in order to be this boring you need to understand other things about the market. Specifically, technical and fundamental indicators. Which for someone new to the markets are about as entertaining a paperclip collection sorted according to size, weight, and colour.

Why am I doing indicators first rather than how the market works? Well this is where you'll either commit or not. It's easy to think you can learn to ignore fear (even as writing this, I had a bad day on the markets and got a little timid), but maths and numbers are a lot more intimidating to learn. Once you learn what things look like on a graph then we can go into how to fill an order for some shares and what to do and when.

I'm not going to treat you like an idiot. So this may be a little overwhelming at first but the information provided may serve you well.

If this chapter feels heavy at any point, skim it now, and return later.

Let's start with what will matter most. The fundamentals.

What are fundamentals you may ask? Simply put they're bits of information you can look at to theorise whether the company is good to invest in, will grow, or will pay a good dividend. Or visa versa.

That leads to the educational part of this book. I'm not going to tell you what to invest in or what to look for but I am going to provide you with probabilities of what each fundamental indicator means.

Every broker you visit will be different and will have different information on it. But these basic ones should be on all.

We'll start with one of the big ones (but also the most complex one in this book so when you're past this you'll be ok). One I mentioned before.

Fundamental Indicators – Look At Me Mum!

P/E as it's simply known, stands for Price to Earnings. At its simplest, it's how much people are willing to pay for one dollar of a company's earnings.

So if a company's share price is $20 and it earns $1 per share in the market. It's P/E is 20.

What does that mean for you?

Well generally (but not always) lower is better. Especially for reinvestment from dividends but this may only apply to well established companies. And just because a company has a low P/E doesn't mean a dividend is coming.

On the flip side, higher can mean the company is growing or popular and lower means the company is cheap and ignored or expected to struggle.

Ultimately you may want to invest in safe companies. Ones that wont disappear. P/E is one small tool for gauging market expectations and potential growth, not safety by itself. With that said. It should be clarified, P/E reflects what the market believes at that point in time not what it will do.

P/E should be looked at historically, to help gauge whether the company is reliable over the long term and not in financial pain. If the P/E fluctuates it may indicate unstable earnings.

It should also be noted, P/E not only changes on earnings but on share price. So if there is a stock market rally P/E will generally (again not always) be higher.

What about Trailing P/E? That's something. It's similar but based on the past using the current share price divided by earnings data from the last 12 months.

What this may explain is how expensive is the company based on what it's already earned.

Markets may not care for yesterday so they often price expectations, past results still matter, but they're not the whole story, so this is something you may use conditionally.

Now onto forward P/E (Are you keeping up? This is a lot I know. Feel free to stop and take your time)

It's similar to trailing P/E. Current share price divided by estimated future earnings, usually from analysts, trends, and company guidance.

The question it may answer is how expensive is this company based on what it might earn.

It can be useful but it is often wrong. Use it conditionally again.

Both trailing and forward P/E are expectations not facts.

Now, the next one is earnings growth. This one is simple. If the company is growing it's generally good. Other investors may expect more of a company but it's up to you how much to expect from what you invest in.

The most important caveat, not to look at the blind numbers but find out why they're growing. Growth without explanation is noise. That's key to a good analysis.

Keep an eye out for accounting tricks vs money from core operations. That matters.

E.g:

Rising earnings + shrinking margins = bad.

Flat earnings + improving margins = good.

Which leads me to debt.

Debt isn't inherently bad, almost all companies have debt. It's debt in context. Debt kills companies in volatile periods but can be helpful when times are good. There is a nuance though. It's important to note that debt amplifies outcomes, good or bad.

If you look at a chart with the debt to equity ratio, some people consider, whether the debt is decreasing, stable, or rising. Alone they aren't proof of anything but just something to consider with other data.

You could also consider interest. Can they cover the interest on their loans with their earnings? Good questions.

That leads to how they invest their earnings and debt (and every other financial matter). This could take some research but is very important. Dumb decisions can mean a dumb company.

I have skipped over so much here regarding fundamentals but these are the bare bones. In fact, P/E is something I probably should have skipped. I just find it a fairly useful tool for myself. Not alone. In conjunction with everything. I think it was worth sharing.

Technical Indicators – Pranks for Nerds

This matters a lot less than you think. In fact, go to the next chapter if you want. This is just something I will list in case you want to consider it in your strategy. I don't place too much weight in it for my long term trades but it could be interesting.

Technical indicators are used in long term trading to assist in finding the optimal time to buy (often there isn't one, sometimes it's luck). But that doesn't mean you should necessarily hold cash forever waiting for the best time. That may never arrive. But that's your choice, it's your money, and I won't tell you what to do with it.

Let's start with RSI. It's a nice little graph which can indicate overbought and oversold conditions. Generally speaking, an RSI of 30 is usually considered oversold by traders, and an RSI of 70 is often considered overbought. When you start trading, have a look at the RSI chart. If you pay attention just because it hits 30 doesn't mean it will go up after. It's just a data point.

Then there's MACD, This one is a little more complex. It indicates momentum and direction. Again it can lie (as all indicators can). It looks complex to understand at first but give it time and research. I find it slightly handy when doing medium term trades but there's not much point in using it long term unless you are intentionally chasing a trend which can be a risky thing to do. Let's put it this way, I don't do that anymore.

Rolling VWAP. I like this one and it will probably be the most useful to you later in your investment days. It in simple terms, indicates short term high and low points. Or in technical, and more correct terms terms, the average price weighted by volume. Traders may use it like a reference line, but I'll be real, It doesn't actually indicate high, and low points, it's just may be simpler to imagine it that way temporarily while you learn how it works. Why is this useful in a long term strategy? Buying at a short term low can (but definitely not always) give you a little extra profit. If you're very lucky that could be 0.5%. Not glamorous, but every little bit helps. Honestly, when you're starting it could better to avoid this and focus on fundamentals. Fundamentals will help you far more and these days, I mostly ignore rolling VWAP long term anyway. The market doesn't play your game.

Supertrends, simply put this one shows you direction of price. Very handy but more suited to medium term trades than the long term trades.

For you, most of these will be unnecessary, but in the long term they are data points for when to buy in and you may consider them as such.

For my risky medium term trades, I use some of them but long term? They really aren't worth the effort in my opinion.

If fundamentals tell you what to own, technicals only hint at when, and even then, they whisper.

Mental Checkpoint

If you’re still reading comfortably, you’re doing fine. Otherwise, take a break.

This book isn’t going anywhere, so take it easy and grab a cup of tea or coffee.

Maybe go for a walk.

Breathe easy, and continue when ready.

Context Beats Numbers – If The World Was Black And White We'd All Be Rich

Oh my. Look at all the fancy things we just heard about. I'm going to be a great success!

Hold up there cowpoke. It's not that simple. There is something called context. Oh no, context, can you just tell me what to do? No. If it was that simple we'd all be rich. There is nuance between the fundamental, and technical indicators, both intertwined, and separate.

Why am I making a sub-chapter for this? Well, it has to be explicitly explained, and very clearly. Nothing, alone from any indicator matters, together they may form a picture, but that picture is dependant on the overall combination of indicators explicitly described by your strategy. Numbers may lie, in my experience, they more often than not do, when you take them in isolated batches. But again, in my experience, when you take them as a larger whole, you get a less appealing but maybe slightly more reliable picture.

We'll go back to P/E for example, the theory is sound of course, but what about when it comes to different industries? The same P/E in different industries can mean different things (we'll use a low P/E of 8 for example). In mining, it could mean they have found a good deposit of say nickle, are successfully mining it, and selling it. This could mean a dividend for you if they are not trying to expand which is also possible. Both of those theoretical situations are good but what suits you better is your decision. Do you want the company to potentially grow for a long term return, or do you want to get a dividend and maybe reinvest it? Up to you. But Just note mining companies tend to be cyclical, they don't always have a constant P/E and remember high and low P/E aren't necessarily bad either way.

In other industries, like IT, the same fake low P/E of 8 could mean they have reliable customers, that pay their bills, the books are good, and they're making money. But a high P/E in IT is often tolerated as it may mean growth is expected.

But it's important to remember about creative accountancy. Have they sold a significant amount of assets recently? Have they done serious cost cutting? Why did they do that? But that could add to the P/E. Is that a sign of a healthy company? Stuff like that you should investigate.

You should also investigate the good stuff as well. Don't just investigate the bad stuff. The good stuff may help determine whether staying with the company is a good thing.

Ask yourself, if you were running a company how would you get your earnings higher, both good and bad ways, and investigate whether the company is acting in the way you would want to for your investment strategy.

Context won't tell you what to do, but it can stop you from doing the wrong thing for the wrong reason.

Comparative Thinking – One Of These Stocks Is Not Like The Other

Remember when you were a kid and you put wooden shapes into a wooden block with cutouts? Well. Let's do that again but this time with adult knowledge.

It may be a good idea to some investors to compare your shapes but this time with stock history, other stocks, and the broader market. Which is what this sub-chapter is about, comparative thinking, the skill of comparing historical data, and potentialities.

So, let's start with company history, this one is potentially the most important if you are currently holding shares in a company. Looking at its past, and future. You may want to look at the earnings the company made in the past, how much debt it has been in recently, earnings growth over time, current sales, whether there has been any dodgy going ons, or creative accounting. This is just good hygiene that you may want to do. I personally check up on it from time to time, but I don't do it every day. You may want to do it differently though.

What about comparing to its peers? Now it should be noted it may be difficult to compare companies in different industries. A mining company doesn't function the same as a biotech company. However, within the same industry, while not perfect, it can be easier to compare to peers. You might want to do this when you're not happy with how a company is performing, or it's breaking your thesis of how it would have performed, but it's generally not a good idea (in the opinion of some investors) to do on a whim. That's just my opinion though.

Another thing you might want to do is compare the company to how the boarder industry or market is performing. If a company is under performing and not meeting your, your thesis, and the markets expectations, you could consider comparing it to the general industry performance historically, and seeing if it aligns. After that you could decide, if you wanted to, reinvest else where in the industry or elsewhere in the market.

It should be reiterated that patience is generally a good thing, a bad few months on the market doesn't necessarily mean a bad stock pick. That said, if you are absolutely sure that you don't want to hold the stock anymore, it might possibly be a good idea for some investors, to look elsewhere for better possibilities.

This is the fundamentals of comparative thinking. It may sound basic, but the skills are hard to master. You might want to think a bit on this from time to time. It's unlikely to hurt.

Quality vs Growth – Neither Is Good Or Bad

I couldn't think of a funny title for this one, so I'm just going to jump right in without a funny analogy that doesn't involve mentioning the ins and outs of the philosophical arguments around the use, of the death ray against every known copy of my awkward school photos.

Now let's get into what I mean by "quality", "quality" by my definition, maybe not yours, is a stable stock with stable growth, that may or may not pay a dividend. "Quality" stocks also tend but not always, to be staples, or institutions which have been around for a long time, have mature management, and have survived a few financial crisis.

Holding "quality" stocks may be useful for stabilising a portfolio, and may (within reason) provide more stability during financial crisis.

None of this is guaranteed of course, and there's pros and cons to a "quality" stock.

We've already suggested a couple of pros for holding "quality" stocks, what about some of the negatives? "Quality" stocks, may not grow quickly, or may not pay a high dividend but sometimes they can pay a reliable dividend.

What about growth stocks? These may be unstable, primarily price-driven, don't pay a dividend, or a small dividend, or an extremely large one off dividend, and the noise you see on the market can swing wildly.

These aren't necessarily bad, but you may want to pay extra attention to them to make sure they're on track.

A well picked growth stock held long term could provide a nice capital boost, but at the same time it should be noted that they may be riskier, maybe even significantly. You may want to consider your risk tolerance before trading, well… any stocks really. And if you're not comfortable with risk you may want to seek independent advice or have someone invest for you, which we discuss in a later chapter.

Most portfolios sit somewhere between quality and growth, not entirely in one camp. Which matters more depends on what your thesis is trying to achieve. As always, you should decide how your portfolio, and thesis is designed.

Earnings vs Cash – Hot Knife Through Butter

Butter. It's delicious and a note so perfect analogy for earnings, and cash. Imagine you're a butter guy, you like butter, you get butter every day from your butter customers, but you have a butter debt you have to pay off cause you got some butter on loan. You give most of your butter to the debt butter people, and you only have a little butter left over to put into the butter bank.

That's earnings vs cash. You may earn a lot but if you're reinvesting it or paying off a debt you may not have a lot of cash in the bank. Now why is this important? While earnings are essential to a continuously functioning company, cash or money in the bank also matters as it can provide a financial buffer for expenses or emergencies without taking on debt which can be dangerous if the wrong emergency occurs.

For example, high interest rates can be risky for a company with debt. If that company has debt, but also quite a bit of cash they can pay off or use that cash as a temporary buffer while they redirect themselves. While cash isn't essential to a well run business, it can be important, and may also be considered by some traders as warning sign.

Early in a companies growth a company may invest in assets more than cash but assets aren't cash and in a crisis assets can be hard to sell. So having some cash can be important.

This is why investors often look at both earnings and cash flow, not just profit. Earnings keep a company alive; cash helps it survive surprises.

Margins – Why This Book Is Easy To Read

Got you there, didn't I? I'm sorry to say, we're not going to talk about page layout, line spacing, and font size. Instead, we're going to talk about financial margins, something you may want to look out for.

Shrinking margins. They tend to be a warning sign. In simple terms it means expenses are starting to increase vs revenue, leading to smaller earnings. This can balloon out especially when debt interest is involved. As you can guess, this isn't usually a good thing, but occasionally there can be legitimate reasons for it. For example, company restructure, or expansion which in the process of they took on significant debt. Both of these things can be disruptive, in which case you may need to research whether it is temporary, or a potentially long term issue regarding a company's shrinking margins. This links back to looking at historical data as well. You may find some use looking, into historical information, as well as current announcements.

Flat revenue is something many investors worry about also but this may matter a lot less. Flat revenue generally means current sales or expenses are consistent, and not growing or shrinking. This isn't good or bad, it just means you may not get any significant growth in the company. That doesn't mean the company isn't growing, or has no changes on costs, or margins, and that may be fine depending on the situation and your thesis. It just may mean it may be slower.

There are a lot of reactions that traders take to flat revenue, some hold, some sell, others buy. Ultimately it comes down to their opinion of the company as a whole.

Debt – Is Good Until It Isn't

Debt. To you, and I on the surface it seems bad. Credit card interest accumulating. You bought a house, and a car, but the payments are killing you. That's somewhat the case with business as well.

In business, sometimes debt can be cheaper than cash. You expand, make more money, pay off the interest, and the debt, and you still keep the income after the debt is paid. This is an example of productive debt. Used responsibly, to grow the business rather than the next example.

Keeping a business afloat with debt is hard, if a company has gotten to that point they may want to try other strategies to build revenue. This may be considered by some traders as a warning sign. When in debt to keep afloat, interest might be paid with the loan itself while trying to get themselves back on track. If they do get themselves solvent, that's great! Congratulations! If they don't the share price (if it hasn't already) may tank, or worse the company may tank.

Low interest rates may also twist the perception of investors when money is cheap. Potentially leading to larger investment even with high debt. This does not mean you should do this. You have to decide yourself if the debt is reasonable enough to invest in. But high debt and interest rate changes may lead to large reactions.

Debt is complex, but it's important to note, debt isn't intrinsically good or bad. It's how it's used, and whether it fits your thesis, that matters.

Now lets get to more boring stuff. The basics of stock markets.

Chapter 5 – Ordering a Pizza

You've got your nibbles, you've eaten them, you're still hungry, now it's time to learn how to order a pizza.

I know, I know, you already know how to order a pizza but do you actually know how to order a few millionths of a pizza? I bet you didn't. That's what this chapter is about.

This book should remain purely informational as you consider your circumstances. We also discuss other investment possibilities in the next chapter, other than the stock market which may be worth a read. This book doesn't focus on them deeply but I would be amiss if I didn't at least mention them.

Now, legal stuff out of the way, how do you place an order (for a pizza). There are 2 or 3 main ways to do that and they all matter for different reasons but we'll get to that soon.

Now, that you have an extremely basic understanding of fundamentals, you can now start looking at stocks. One option is to start with companies you know, then pick your companies and categorise them by industry, choose from that list a diverse selection of stocks with different industries one of the primary selection criteria, add them to a nice simple list and start to research into them for safety and profitability. Just one possible, way of starting your stock journey.

This is called diversification and is commonly considered by many investors as good idea for risk-management as industries also rise and fall at different rates on the market, and can reduce damage, but it still doesn't prevent losses. Some industries are impacted by metal and ore prices, others by consumer sentiment, and every industry will change drastically on different days, weeks, and months.

So why diversify? It generally reduces loss if one industry is greatly impacted by an event or market sentiment.

So it's generally a good idea for some investors and traders, depending on your circumstances.

OK. So you've chosen a few companies and researched into them. If you haven't, do so now. It won't hurt and it's good practice. Doesn't mean you should act, it's just nice to have a look.

Only, once you think you're ready, and confident you may have enough information to continue, and you're possibly ready to invest.

Am I saying you're ready now? No definitely not, please read the rest of the book and do your research then decide.

This is a good page by the way, because we're now going to get into types of orders.

Generally speaking, there are 3 main order types when buying and selling.

- Market

- Limit
- Conditional Order at Market or Limit

So what are each of those?

Let's start with the simplest. Market order.

Simply, you're just placing an order and having it fill at any price but hopefully at the best available price at that moment.

This is generally common if you're buying/selling small amounts, you don't care about getting a certain price, you're trading during market hours, and you want an instant trade rather than waiting for it to fill. Market orders are commonly used when starting out as a beginner. Many beginners to do such.

Of course making any trade depends on a significant range of factors like, liquidity, spreads, spread size, and volatility.

Second is the limit order, which is useful when you want or need to buy at a specific price. This may be useful for buying or selling large amounts of shares, buying or selling off market (riskier), and you don't mind waiting. The downside is your trade isn't guaranteed to fill or may partially fill. Meaning the trade isn't guaranteed to execute. It's a handy order type but you need to know it's conditional (as with all of them).

Speaking of conditional. There's another order type called a conditional order. This might be used if you want to automate certain orders at points/conditions. You set a few conditions and it places a predefined order the moment those conditions trigger. Sounds good right? Well it has a caveat. When that triggers you're added to the queue of trades at that moment. It could fill fast or messy. Messy means it could mean fill worse or inconsistently if price is moving fast. It's just the price you pay for keeping a small secret. It's not really that simple though, as there are many other things that impact your order filling, like price-time priority, venue rules, and order type, but that's outside the scope of this book. I'm sure you can see the use in this but quite often there isn't. When it comes to small amounts, it could come down to personal preference.

Just remember, markets go up and down. Some months or years you'll lose money, others you'll gain it. When I said long term trading it is a very long game. Don't assume just because the price is going down that it's doing bad. That's why you keep an eye on the fundamentals. Stay calm. Analyse. And make your own decisions. It's never black and white like your ape brain or the red and green numbers say.

On top of that, just a quick note on tax. Tax is generally only triggered when you sell, not while you hold, but rules vary depending on a few factors so check, and do some research yourself.

Dividends are also usually taxed in the year you receive them; franking credits can also offset tax depending on your circumstances. They can reduce the tax you pay on dividends, and in some cases are refundable. Pretty cool hey? You may want to do some research into that as if you're holding long term you may get a few dividends.

Wow. Writing this there isn't much else to say other than it typically takes 2 business days (research T+2) after the order you placed for your shares to materialise. Depending on market and broker of course. That's called settlement. You can still trade while settlement is happening but it's important to note that when you order them, is just a promise of shares until settlement is complete. Then you own them or if you sell them, don't own them.

I should mention, settlement rules may vary by market and broker. So keep that in mind when doing your research.

Anyway, the stock market, while I'm not going to say it's simple, the actual action of trading pretty close to simple. Isn't that cool? But isn't it a trap?

If it's so easy to place an order (and you can before you've settled it), it means it's just as easy to react to your emotions.

I think I've covered the main traps so far so I'm not going to preach to you. So, I guess this is the page where you go off and do your own research.

Money Back Not Guaranteed

No joke about this one. Just the title. It's a serious topic with serious implications. Is this something you will encounter? Maybe, so read on.

Liquidity on markets is usually high, but during times of stress, especially with small caps, you may not be able to sell your shares at the price you want, or in the worst case, at all.

What do I mean by this? Imagine, everyone is trying to sell, but very few are trying to buy a stock, people are willing to settle for less, and less to sell, but you want to sell at a certain price to keep yourself happy enough.

This is where your money back guarantee fails. You could sell, with a market order, and take a potentially risky, unstable, and/or large loss. You could hope, and pray it goes back up, but this is holding the bag, and may not suit your strategy and thesis.

This is not something that always happens but it's common enough that it needs to be described to you. Stress in markets happens, and awareness is essential.

If this happens, and you're not sure what to do you may want to talk to a financial adviser, or accountant. It can be very psychologically, and or financially taxing to fix things like this.

That's not a legal disclaimer by the way. That's honestly what I might do if I couldn't handle the situation. It's a good default to have in my opinion.

Sometimes delegating, or getting a second opinion can help you out of a situation.

What You See Is Not What You Get

"Look at me, this number is good. Very good. Me want number." says the ape brain.

"That is actually a very good number. It matches my thesis, and I approve after careful consideration." disclaims the human brain

You place an order.

"AAAAGAGAGGHHH NUMBER BAD!!!" screams the ape brain.

"Yeah bad trade… what happened?" questions the human brain.

That could have been one of the many small things you may encounter when placing a trade.

Let's start with slippage. Slippage is the difference between the price you expect to trade at and the price the order fills at. This can happen for many reasons. You're looking at the last price, and using a market order. Which doesn't necessarily, use the last listed price to fill your order. When using a market order it will use what the market is asking for.

When buying shares via market order it will use the order book and calculate how many shares you can buy in an attempt to give the best price. This is the ask side of the order book. If there are too many shares to buy for one price, it may go to the next best price, and do a fill at 2 or more different prices. This will give you an average price, which is most of the time included on your trade confirmation anyway.

However, when selling shares via market order it will try and do the same thing. This time on the bid side of the order book.

These are examples, of slippage.

Other than that, there is timing. You don't have a direct line to your stock exchange, and most of the time your broker will try and be as accurate as it can but it can't always keep everything perfectly up to date. So sometimes when you place a trade you could miss it because of timing due to technological constraints. It's just life on the stock market, and you should be aware that it happens.

Lastly, there is opportunity erosion. This is one that you have to treat with extreme scepticism, as it can go both ways. Sometimes, you place a limit order too low, and you miss the rush. Cool, no problems. It may go down later in the day, week, or month, or not for years. That's OK. Missed it. You may consider moving on. Or if it still meets your thesis, you could buy in at the higher price, if your thesis allows lower margins.

For example, today, I did a trade just like this. My thesis wasn't broken and I was happy to take 1% less profit, and the extra potential loss was within thesis guidelines.

My thought process behind this was:

My thesis was aiming for more but if my thesis maintains its integrity, I will still be happy to take any profit or loss I make.

I don't stress, and I take decisions like that logically. It was only 5 minutes at the time, but that was enough time to go through my notes, make a decision, and take 2 minutes break to think about it.

Not ideal behaviour in my opinion, but my theses while well defined, maintain flexibility for the occasional situation where this may be required. Having a well defined, and flexible thesis, allowed me to do what I needed to, without strategy/thesis drift. Doesn't mean you should do this immediately. It takes a lot of self knowledge, and control to do this semi-reliably. Emotion can still come into play. We're all still human.

The thing you might consider important is not to make snap decisions. Making snap decisions in my opinion, usually leads to bad trades. So I keep my thesis in mind at all times.

Most of what I said, in my opinion, focuses on short, and medium term trades. Which you may want to play around with much later down the track. But although potentially they have better profit, they also may have greater risk, and loss. They can also have greater psychological, emotional, and financial damage. So going straight into these may not be the best idea. This information, might not be important for you now, but it's worth researching, and considering.

Why Fair Value Is A Comfort Story

Fair value. It sounds great doesn't it? Undervalued? It's gotta rise. Overvalued, it's gotta fall?

Fair value doesn't always mean much at all in the grand scheme of things. It's just another data point.

Share prices can continue to rise in markets with great confidence. Perhaps for years. Others can fall for months or years, also with or without explanation.

Fair value is just what analysts think the stock is worth. It isn't a prediction or any real indication of value. The value of a stock is set by the market. Personal value however, is set by yourself. You may want to give it your own tangible or intangible value based on what you think but it may not be a good idea to get attached to a stock or share unless you decide you want to have a vested interest in their mission. That's up to you though, but some traders will tell you that having a non-financial interest is a bad idea. A healthy balance might be suitable for investors with an ethics based trading style.

I think we went off topic there, but it's an interesting discussion to have.

Loss vs Recovery Time – It's Just Not Fair...

Loss happens every day on the stock market. Some lose big, others small. Did you know however, that loss takes longer to recover from especially when compounding profit?

It's just a sad reality of mathematics. Especially, if you integrate compounding interest/dividends into your strategy. Which may or may not be a good idea depending on how you design your strategy.

That said even if you just hold your shares without reinvesting, the higher they are, the higher the daily percentage drop means, and the less the percentage rise means.

In short, while this doesn't sound good on paper, it's a reality of trading. All investors have to deal with this. The only thing that doesn't that I can think of at the moment, is compounding interest in a bank account. Which according to many investors, is a very safe thing to do.

In my opinion, it's the safest thing to do. It's just potentially lower interest.

Fees For Months – Is That Actually a Problem?

Remember when you made that buy order, and you got charged a fee? While that may not matter too much in the long term, it may not be a good idea to ignore it entirely.

There are usually two fees, one when filling a buy order, one when filling a sell order. Usually, the fees are based on how much you're trading. Whether that is a flat fee, or variable fee based on a percentage of your order. It is important to know what fees your broker assigns.

If you decide your strategy involves taking a certain percentage rather than long term holding you may want to take fees into account. I think that's an excellent idea as at lower amounts the fees can be a high percentage of your trade.

Interestingly, if you decide to compound your results, or increase your position, flat fees based on trade value may increase or decrease as a percentage of your trade as your trading value rises or falls.

Yes, even trading too much may make your fees higher than they were before. Usually it's important to factor in fees when determining your trading amount, and thesis.

E.g. with my broker, which isn't the cheapest but I like it, I pay $9.95 AUD per order under $1000 AUD. As I approach $1000 AUD as my order value that $9.95 gets closer to 1% of my order value rather than the roughly 2% it would be if I traded the minimum order of $500 AUD.

If however, I reach $1000 AUD or go over it, I pay 14.95 per order. This is still cheaper than the minimum order (roughly 1.5% vs 2%) but when you do the math, you pay less fees when below $1000 AUD but reaching the threshold.

The big question is, does it suit your strategy to trade with less but less fees? Does that extra $5 AUD matter enough to your trades to warrant less capital in the market?

That's the big question. As mentioned, if you're trading over years you may decide not to care. But if you decide to trade over months you might decide to think about fees.

Exit Stage Left

This is just a small expansion on "money back not guaranteed", and a small sub-chapter to end chapter 5.

Remember when I said liquidity is not always guaranteed? There's a very simple reason for this.

Most trades are someone else making an exit. That's one of the main influencing factors in determining the bid and ask prices in the order book, and also the last price. Usually the last price is the last trade executed, and that's usually someone buying or selling an order of shares. I mean, those shares usually have to come from somebody. Hence why it influences the price. The price usually rises when more people are buying than people selling (but not always). There's always a trade of shares though.

Also Just note just because people are exiting doesn't necessarily mean you should. You might want to do some research, check the news, and market announcements if you're worried.

Let's get into the difference between some of the many different ways of investing.

Mental Checkpoint

You’re still here? Awesome!

Take a break now if you want. You’ve read a lot of dense content.

You’re going excellent.

Chapter 6 – Stockholder Karen and Her Blue Cheese

"I own the company! Now give me that blue cheese!!!" demanded Karen as she abused a poor defenceless supermarket employee.

Don't be like Karen… While technically true when you buy shares your opinion, and right to blue cheese isn't.

Joking aside, that's the long, and short of what happens when you buy shares. You usually buy a representation of a very small section of the company. You don't get a stock certificate generally.

Now you might be like Karen right now, and not even know it.

There are three ways you are exposed to the stock market, and at least in Australia most people will have some exposure to super, whether they meant to or not.

1. Owning shares (Buying shares which this book is mostly about)
2. Having exposure to shares (Managed funds, and the such)
3. Having outcomes linked to shares (Superannuation, if you're an Aussie you've probably heard of this one)

Let's break these down into the pros, and cons of each.

When you buy shares directly like talked about in this book, you:

- Own a legal interest in the company/become a share holder
- Have voting rights on the companies actions (usually negligible in practice, but if many people other than you agree on things, voting rights can add up)

- Bear full responsibility for your decisions

In short:

Control of your money is high, responsibility is high, and most importantly, and much the point of this book, cognitive load is high. You're dealing with your own decisions, and as discussed will have good, and bad days within your mind.

Now, onto managed funds, these are good where you mostly want to set, and forget, but not give up full control. If you have been intimidated by this book so far you may want to consider this (or the next) option but that's ultimately up to you. It's a crazy world the finance world. Sometimes, the better decision may be to let others handle it. Which is why I'm adding this section.

Right, managed funds. In managed funds you:

- Do not choose the companies invested in
- Cannot veto decisions
- You may own units in a managed fund rather than companies themselves.
- Someone else re-balances, allocates your capital, and manages risk according to their mandate.

Low to medium control, but a reasonable distance from decisions.

For a clear example of control: you have a choice of funds, may have a choice of risk level, and may be able to withdraw your money when needed.

In other words: You're outsourcing decisions, and mistakes.

Lastly, there's superannuation, which is generally, tax-advantaged, locked away from access, and managed for you, but you can generally choose your risk profile, and sometimes asset mix. You do not choose individual investments, timing, or changes.

Very low control, and very low responsibility.

But that may be appropriate for you. Only you can choose which one suits you, if any.

In superannuation, and managed funds should note you own units in a pool (or an interest), rather than holding shares in your own name. Structures can vary though.

Again, it could be a good idea to dismiss this book now. People panic less when they have less control, but on the flip side blame others (like investors) more easily, usually stay invested longer because managing your own shares isn't for everyone, and as such managed products are for many people. Not because they're necessarily optimal, but because they reduce errors, mistakes, and responsibility.

No method discussed here is superior in all cases, different people, and nuances matter.

The best method is one you can understand, emotionally tolerate, and won’t sabotage you. That last one is most important. Knowing ones self is most important when investing.

Can You Just Do It?

Sometimes this is the easiest decision, and I wouldn't blame you for it. Doing something like investing yourself may carry risk, and having a professional do everything for you just may make your life easier, and over the long term may even be more stable or profitable (but obviously no guarantees).

This sub-chapter will be short, but will have a few good points.

Delegation can be a solid risk management strategy. If you know that you're not going to be able to handle many of the things in this book. You might consider getting someone else to do it for you. Whether that's a managed fund, your superannuation, or just talking to a financial adviser about what you could do. They're all potential options.

You may feel obligated to do it yourself, and there are pros and cons to that. There's no shame in delegating. Remember your circumstances matter more than anything in this book. There are plenty of potential paths to a brighter financial future. How they eventuate depends on a range of factors including yourself. Having someone else do it may be the sane solution for many people.

The Difference Between Access and Opportunity

Opportunity, it's all that most of us ever want. Sadly, there are conditions to opportunity, many which I have discussed, maybe not directly, but they are in the book.

Your opportunities, may be limited for a variety of reasons. Commonly these can include, time, financial, education, legal, or anything that is common in life.

Even though access to the stock market these days can be as easy as signing up online, and maybe (depending on the broker) going into the provider themselves to give ID, the availability of opportunity is the limiting factor.

I'm not saying your circumstances make it impossible, but they can make it harder.

I know mine are hard, living on 30k AUD a year, and building for my retirement? Sounds mad. I know it does to me. But it's not impossible.

If there are friends, and family that are willing to support you. Please let them help. There is no shame in that especially if you are being responsible in their eyes.

The main thing is that you don't take advantage of that support, and reciprocate where you can.

That's simple common sense life advice that I shouldn't have given out, but there's a fine line between receiving support, and taking too much that can be easily broken.

Have pride, just know when to pull back and accept support. That's the hard part.

Chapter 7 – Zen or Stingy, You Decide

Going with less… it's not generally considered human nature. We like things. We're just featherless magpies when it comes down to it. Mainly cause we squawk a lot, and like shiny things like wedding rings.

Pretty normal when it comes down to it. The next question is, can you be happy with numbers being your shiny thing? Well maybe you should consider a little life simplification. It's not for everyone though. It can definitely be hard when you have kids. The well being and nutrition of your family (if you have one) have to come first.

Enter the pizza gambit again. This was one of the 2 big things I had to give up to make everything I've been writing about in this book happen. The other was alcohol. Both I really do love. Both are relaxation things for me.

That said, abstinence and denial can be unsustainable. So instead of going hard like I did, do something sensible like limit yourself to an engorging day once a month. Living life without the simple pleasures isn't life at all.

I'm going to clarify everything I've just said now with a stipulation, that this is not life advice. Everyone's situation is different, and the world is incredibly nuanced. What you do need to do is take into consideration your circumstances and plan for them.

Don't want to give up your beer? That's fine. Make a compromise or plan, adapt, and change, life is very fluid, and treating it rigidly leads to burnout (I know this for a fact).

Break your plan significantly? No problems. Forgive yourself, and learn you lessons and move on. Blaming yourself isn't productive in the slightest but it's very easy to do.

The most important thing to remember is you're in this for the long term. Money comes and goes, especially in the stock market, but also in life.

Mostly rambling now but the point I am trying to make now is, we're all human, and as long as you're doing your best for your circumstances you're doing OK. You don't have to be a saint of financial saving, just do your best.

In a world which is increasingly tense, with increasing expectations of productivity, and success, understanding that your own health, either physical, emotional, or daily financial, matters more than anything in this book is important. This book is a bonus, showing a mindset, and a potential path forward, not a secret to anything.

You Gotta Be Good To Yourself – Life Without Comfort Isn’t Life At All

Deprivation of nice things is not always good. We’ve discussed this. But have you actually considered it as an asset for your portfolio?

Really, no kidding. Whether using a paper or digital portfolio, you may want to add a note every week telling yourself what you did to treat yourself that week.

If you find yourself without a history of kind, friendly notes telling yourself about the good things about your life, you may need to change your habits.

For example, today I got a coffee, and Thai food for both myself and my neighbour. That went into the portfolio notes.

Small things that make you happy can increase your sustainability as an investor, reduce your stress, and give you something other than numbers, and sacrifice.

Deprivation backfires. It can make you emotional, stressed, increase your expectations of yourself, and the market (which you can’t control).

Maybe reducing the raw numbers, and cash invested will help you in the long term.

It’s a hard lesson to learn sometimes. One, I’m still working on myself. But I always write my good news notes.

Chapter 8 – Traveller’s Guide to The Stock Market

DON'T FREAKOUT said a famous book in big letters on the back, which I may or not have read at some point with a large smile on my face.

Best advice I could ever have received. If I believed it at the time…

Well… I've taken it on board now. Let's look a bit into the common causes of stock market panic.

If you start trading on the markets, you'll have red days. Where the numbers go down, and you might panic.

Take it easy, panicking often results in poor decisions which may lead to loss. Check what you have invested in. Is it a small cap? Has it gone down 5% today? It may just be stock market noise. Is it a large cap? Also it may be noise. Stuff quite often means nothing, or is reactionary to some temporary news. So maybe look at your fundamentals and thesis, if you're worried. But what I do is, I don't over analyse, don't panic, don't immediately react. My opinion is bad decisions are bad.

In fact when you're worried, get a cup of calming herbal tea. It's delicious, it's a calming ritual for many, and having something in your hands while sipping it is psychologically calming. It's the same reason why some people say coffee is calming (it's not).

But yeah, stay calm, if you make the right decision for yourself you'll be fine as you'll know it was the right decision for yourself (even if at the time).

But what about quiet days? They can be just as worrying. Why isn't my stock moving for weeks? Sometimes they do that. It's also one of the best possible scenarios. It's stable, but if you want something that grows in price, that's up to you. But make sure you plan ahead, make sure it fits into your strategy, maths, and portfolio. I personally, have a couple of stocks which are flat or falling right now. Am I worried? Not really, because they aren't going anywhere. That's up to you though, but chasing profits has traditionally been riskier than the alternative, but if a company no longer fits your thesis and strategy that's the time some investors might want to consider redirecting your investment elsewhere.

What about your thesis? It's not behaving like you expect? Ok, That's fine. You might want to take a break, a day or 2, and reconsider your investments but reactionary trading is not a good thing as a rule. Your money still exists as a share, make your decision with a clear and calm mind.

Drawdowns, as in the price is falling? That could be fine also, as long as nothing is broken in your thesis.

Doubt? Take a break. You're probably freaking out.

Sitting in the chair, go outside and touch some grass. Really... You've been there too long.

Staying invested emotionally and psychologically is risky as when you watch the market rise and fall you could make a snap decision. Time to calm down is important before any decision. You're not a day trader, take your time, relax with a cup of tea, and analyse when you have some spare time.

If you're feeling significant emotion, consider stepping back. You don't always make good decisions when you're emotional.

Oh, and don't trade or invest because you're bored. While this doesn't always go wrong, it's not a great idea.

I should also mention that regret comes in both directions. Quite often from selling too early or holding too long. Selling too early isn't necessarily a bad thing. If you make a profit, that's good news, any profit is good profit (and I mean that and truly believe that from personal experience), if you don't there's nothing you can do, and chasing/dwelling on it won't usually help much.

Both forms of regret are survivable, they may feel overwhelming at first but in time you'll learn to understand that's just your ape brain worrying about the short term.

Next comes the myth of validation, and bias.

Never, expect the market to go your way, expect both profit, and loss but never consistency. Never, expect answers to why either, you can tell yourself this is why that happened but you probably won't know. Professionals have trouble as well. You can expect this with any trading or investing you do.

I didn't mean to lecture you here, but this is one of the most important parts of the book. Your safety and health are your #1 priority.

Why Someone Always Thinks They're Smarter Than You

The big lie of the stock market is ego. It can cause, mistakes, bias, and everyone to be annoyed with you, but it can also be used for manipulation.

I won't go into ego in regards to yourself, and how to stop it. If you've read this book, this far I don't think you have to worry about that just yet.

What I'll go into is, how ego, confidence, and fake confidence can be used against you.

Confidence is a great motivating force. If someone is confident you're more likely to believe them. Which is why market advice is so risky to provide. Confidence doesn't guarantee results as much as you or they may believe them.

Fake confidence, is even riskier. The internet is a good place for examples. While not all advice on the internet is bad, in fact there is some very good advice, some use confidence or fake confidence to attempt to tip the market conditions in their favour so they can make a profit.

Usually, this requires mass scale, or a reasonably sized audience, and is washed away by numerous disclaimers.

The other thing to look out for is ego. Just because someone has had success doesn't mean they'll have success with your money. Ego and overconfidence is often punished on the stock market, as adaptation, and changes in the markets happen all the time.

One strategy that works one day may not work the next.

Chapter 9 – Reality Is Not A Prison, Your Plan Is

Life… It's great isn't it? However, you should expect a few curve balls.

Dam… it's over isn't it. Life has hit the fan, and there's nothing left to do but divest.

It's not over though. Life can get in the way, and that's OK. If that happens you can come back to your or a new plan when you want to.

I've definitely done that a few times in my early trading career. When I had my first 10k invested… well, my car died. No point in recovering it so… well… I had to divest. Life happens.

It could be anything that causes you to leave, and that's okay. Forgive yourself. Illness, job loss, family, needs, even your own mental health from trading or investing. They all are valid reasons to leave.

On a more technical stand point, your thesis or strategy may not meet your needs anymore. These changes can be slow, boring, and opaque. Certainty is rare. Maybe in that case exiting the market may be worth considering to some investors. You may want to reenter, you may not. That's your decision.

Time is also an exit risk. It can reduce some risks as we have discussed, but also it can lead to complacency, and neglect.

You may want to ask yourself, what is the difference between patience and stubbornness. Some investors may want to consider this from time to time.

Some investments end in profit, some end flat, some end in loss.

Others end loud, or quietly, many end because you've changed.

The Myth of The Perfect Re-Entry III – Revenge of the Market

OK. You've left the market. Probably for good reason. Now you want to get back in. Guess what? It's unlikely you're going to find a perfect entry or re-entry.

What do I mean? Well, before I got back into the market after buying my car, I was waiting for a perfect moment. Clarity from self doubt. It's unlikely there will be any. Sometimes you gotta bite the bullet, get your friends, and family to promise you a pizza (optional), and get in there.

I'll give you an example. When I got back in long term, I bought some shares, I thought they would go up soon, as my thesis described that as a possibility. But nope they dropped 6%, and this was a pretty well known stock in Australia. That's OK. I knew it would be choppy. Right now is a crazy time for global markets. Nothing is guaranteed at the time of writing this.

But I digress, the point I was trying to make is a perfect re-entry is mostly a myth. You would have to be very lucky to get the perfect entry, and that's OK. If you do, celebrate.

That's talking technically though.

What about the question, if you're emotionally ready? Well that's up to you. The human mind is messy. You can be scared of something, and still want to do it. That's not an easy thing to overcome.

You have to decide, whether you are emotionally ready enough to reenter the market. If not, talking to an independent adviser may be a good idea. They may offer ideas, and services you may have not considered previously which may help.

You can always reenter later, if you want to, most of the time there will be nothing stopping you. Just take care of yourself.

Life Vs Market – The Battle For The Ages

Ding, ding, goes the bell. Life, and the stock market are going in for the belt.

You may not want to let either win. Personal instability can matter more than market volatility.

When I was day trading, I spent every free waking hour, monitoring the market with unrealistic goals of 3% that week.

It made me stressed, mildly paranoid, reactionary, and all sorts of other bad things.

Boy, that seems silly in hindsight. You’ve got to have a life.

That’s why I have to stress, the life vs market balance.

Hopefully, you never have to encounter that issue, but you may at some point. You’re probably most at risk when you just start trading, but constant obsession, and monitoring just isn’t worth it.

Here’s some things you might want to do to manage yourself, if you’re worried about your life balance, or see some warning signs you don’t like.

1. Write in a book when you will check the markets. If you're checking them constantly, you might want to only check them once a day, and then revisit after a month as that gives you some time to adapt.

2. Try to keep an eye on your mindset, are you getting stressed? You might want to take a break, or make a cup of tea. Small things.

3. Write in your journal, thoughts, feelings, and trades. Trade journals are often used by professionals, and can provide long term insight, into how you are feeling or if your emotions are impacting your trades. Just don't lie to yourself. That probably won't help.

Market life balance may seem like a trivial life skill but it's a skill which many traders may never learn.

Chapter 10 – Pickles! The Food Of The Future!

Purely theoretical, until it happened. Just like the pickle. Food of the future. Tasty for some, disgusting for others, pickles really do represent the concept of the future. When did the pickle happen? We don't know, just like the future which sneaks up on us.

Everything in this chapter is purely theoretical, as you can't predict the future, and should be considered as educational only.

Let us start with the elephant in the room, the big boogeyman at the time of writing this book. Artificial Intelligence & Automation. This could make this book pointless. Why? If AI and automation become exactly what some of the CEOs of those companies are saying it will be, it could completely remove the need for a stock market, or capitalist economy, and could change how economies are structured, which could change what investment even looks like, due to an economic management shift. This is all extremely speculative though. Yet the question remains, why again?

Well, AI and Automation may create a gradual displacement of human labour across all forms of jobs, decoupling work from income, making prices, and returns smaller and cheaper, but not without potential economic disruption from unemployment, etc. It's also important to note productivity gains may not translate evenly into wages, leading to increased pressure on taxation systems, social security, and consumer demand. This is likely to be a long transition rather than suddenly happening but it is good to consider.

Employment structures have changed over time as well, with the growth of contract, gig, and fragmented work, reduced job stability and predictable income, it may be harder for individuals to plan long term contributions, and hence an increase in importance of a personal financial buffer. I'm not going to predict the future, but this may accelerate in the future as companies continue to look to cut costs. Which isn't always sustainable.

Another point to discuss is the worlds ageing demographic, the lower birth rates, increased dependency ratio, and strain on social security. This may be temporary as the population statistics correct themselves but many countries require population growth to maintain productivity. This is a catch 22 in many ways, you need population to maintain productivity, you need a good cost of living to maintain birth rates, you need birth rates to maintain productivity long term, you need good productivity to maintain tax revenue. Currently, while writing this book this is a big problem in many countries.

You've also got geopolitical instability, but that happens all the time, not to dismiss it. It's highly important. It happens and you have to consider it in your decision making.

The point I am trying to make is, long term strategies must tolerate, interruptions, and disruptions into the future. Can you guarantee that? No. Definitely not. It's a crazy unpredictable world, and as of writing we're going into an exciting, and scary new technological revolution which may upset a lot of things.

Take a chance if you want, but have a think about what the future may hold. It's ultimately up to you.

Closing Statement

If you've made it this far, you already know this book was never about pizza.
Pizza was just the excuse. A small, harmless reward for doing something that's actually uncomfortable: thinking long-term, sitting with uncertainty, and learning not to panic when the numbers don't behave.

This book didn't give you a strategy because strategies age badly.
It didn't give you certainty because certainty doesn't exist. What it tried to give you was something far less exciting and far more useful: a way to think. You've seen that markets don't reward cleverness as often as they punish impatience.

- That doing nothing can be an action.
- That fear feels urgent but rarely is.
- That numbers matter, but context matters more, and that the biggest risk most people face isn't volatility, leverage, or timing, it's themselves.

If there's a single thread running through every chapter, it's this:
you don't need to be brilliant, fast, or right all the time. You just need to be kind to yourself, patient enough to stay in the game, and disciplined enough not to sabotage your own future.

- You will make mistakes.
- You will doubt yourself.

- You will sometimes sell too early, hold too long, or do nothing when action might have helped.

That's not failure, that's participation.

This book isn't here to turn you into a trader, an investor, or a numbers person. It's here to help you build resilience in a system that doesn't care how confident you feel on the day. To remind you that life will interrupt your plans, and that stepping away is not quitting.
And to show you that progress doesn't have to look dramatic to be real.

- If you close this book and decide to do nothing, fine.

- If you take one idea and discard the rest, also fine.

- If this sits on a shelf for ten years before it makes sense, honestly, that might be ideal.

Just remember: there's no perfect entry, no final answer, and no finish line. There's only your circumstances, your decisions, and how well you treat yourself while navigating them, and if, somewhere along the way, you hit a goal, big or small, I hope you celebrate it with something meaningful but inconsequential.

Like pizza.

Made in the USA
Monee, IL
04 November 2026

67380109R00066

Pierre Kalmar

est membre du cercle littéraire

Catherine de Médicis

Ce livre appartient à